Better Homes and Gardens®

FRESH GARDEN RECIPES

Our seal assures you that every recipe in *Fresh Garden Recipes*
has been tested in the Better Homes and Gardens® Test Kitchen.
This means that each recipe is practical and reliable, and
meets our high standards of taste appeal.

For years, Better Homes and Gardens® Books has been a leader in publishing cook books. In *Fresh Garden Recipes,* we've pulled together a delicious collection of recipes from several of our latest best-sellers. These no-fail recipes will make your cooking easier and more enjoyable.

Editor: Elizabeth Woolever
Editorial Project Manager: Mary Helen Schiltz
Graphic Designer: Harijs Priekulis
Electronic Text Processor: Paula Forest

On the front cover: Zucchini and Tomato Parmesan (see recipe, page 28)

Contents

Chicken Florentine with Baby Carrots

2 whole medium chicken breasts, skinned, boned, and halved lengthwise
Salt and pepper
2 tablespoons cooking oil
½ cup chopped onion
2 cloves garlic, minced
2 teaspoons cornstarch
1¼ cups milk
½ of a 3-ounce package cream cheese, cut up
2 tablespoons dry white wine
1 pound fresh spinach, stems removed
8 ounces fresh baby carrots *or* 4 medium carrots, bias-sliced into 1-inch pieces

● Sprinkle chicken with salt and pepper. In a large skillet brown chicken in hot oil about 12 minutes or just till tender, turning once. Remove from skillet, reserving drippings. For sauce, cook onion and garlic in reserved drippings till tender. Stir in cornstarch. Add milk all at once. Cook and stir till thickened and bubbly; cook and stir for 2 minutes more. Stir in cheese till it melts. Remove from heat. Stir in wine.

● Rinse spinach in water. In a large saucepan cook spinach, covered, in just the water that clings to the leaves. Reduce the heat when steam forms, then cook, covered, about 3 minutes or till spinach is tender. Drain well; squeeze out excess liquid. Cook carrots in a small amount of boiling water for 2 to 3 minutes or till crisp-tender; drain.

● Arrange cooked spinach in 4 individual casseroles. Place chicken on spinach; pour sauce over the chicken. Add carrots. Seal, label, and freeze.

● **To serve,** bake 1 or more frozen casseroles, loosely covered, in a 375° oven 50 to 60 minutes or till heated through. Sprinkle with paprika and garnish with small spinach leaves, if desired. Makes 4 single-serving entrées.

Cashew Chicken

¼ cup soy sauce
¼ cup dry sherry
1 tablespoon quick-cooking tapioca, finely crushed
1 teaspoon sugar
½ teaspoon grated gingerroot
¼ teaspoon crushed red pepper
1 tablespoon cooking oil
2 medium carrots, thinly bias sliced
1 medium green pepper, cut into ¾-inch pieces
1 small onion, cut into wedges
2 whole medium chicken breasts, skinned, boned, and cut into 1-inch pieces
Cashews

● For sauce, stir together soy sauce, sherry, tapioca, sugar, gingerroot, pepper, and ⅔ cup *water.* Set aside. Preheat a wok or large skillet over high heat; add oil. (Add more oil as necessary during cooking.) Stir-fry carrots, green pepper, and onion in hot oil for 2 minutes. Remove from wok.

● Add *half* of the chicken to the hot wok. Stir-fry for 2 minutes. Remove from wok. Stir-fry remaining chicken for 2 minutes. Return all chicken to wok. Push chicken from center of wok. Stir sauce; add to wok. Cook and stir till bubbly; cook and stir for 2 minutes more. Remove from the heat. Stir in vegetables; cool. Spoon into 4 individual casseroles. Seal, label, and freeze.

● **To serve,** bake 1 or more frozen casseroles, covered, in a 375° oven for 35 to 40 minutes or till heated through. Or place one portion of the frozen mixture in a small saucepan. Cover and cook over medium-low heat for 15 to 20 minutes or till heated through, stirring occasionally. Sprinkle with cashews. Makes 4 single-serving entrées.

Chicken Florentine with
Baby Carrots

Vegetable-Stuffed Steaks

Stuffed shirts, stockings, spuds . . . and now steak!

2 beef top loin steaks,
    cut 1 inch thick
    (about 1 pound total)
    Nonstick spray coating
1 cup sliced fresh mushrooms
2 tablespoons chopped onion
2 tablespoons chopped green
    pepper
2 tablespoons shredded
    carrot
1 small clove garlic, minced
¼ teaspoon Worcestershire
    sauce
    Dash dried thyme, crushed

● Make a pocket in each steak by cutting horizontally into the steak from one side almost to the opposite side. Spray a saucepan with nonstick coating. Add mushrooms, onion, green pepper, carrot, garlic, Worcestershire sauce, and thyme. Cook and stir about 4 minutes or till vegetables are tender.

● Fill each steak pocket with half of the mushroom mixture. Place steaks on a rack in an unheated broiler pan. Broil 4 inches from the heat till desired doneness, turning once. (Allow 16 to 18 minutes total time for medium-rare.) Makes 4 servings.

Southern-Style Round Steak

Sweet potatoes lend a special Southern charm.

1½ pounds beef round steak,
    cut about ¾ inch thick
    Nonstick spray coating
3 medium sweet potatoes *or*
    yams, peeled and sliced
    ½ inch thick
1 large onion, cut into thin
    wedges
1 medium green pepper, cut
    into ½-inch strips
1 16-ounce can tomatoes,
    cut up
1 teaspoon sugar
½ teaspoon dried thyme,
    crushed
⅛ teaspoon pepper
    Several dashes bottled hot
    pepper sauce
1 tablespoon cornstarch
1 tablespoon cold water

● Cut meat into six serving-size pieces; pound to ¼- to ½-inch thickness. Sprinkle lightly with salt and pepper. Spray a Dutch oven with nonstick coating. Brown meat, half at a time, in the Dutch oven. Return all meat to Dutch oven. Top with sweet potatoes, onion, and green pepper. Stir together *undrained* tomatoes, sugar, thyme, pepper, and hot pepper sauce. Pour over meat and vegetables.

● Cover and bake in a 350° oven for 1¼ to 1½ hours or until meat and vegetables are tender, occasionally spooning sauce over mixture. With a slotted spoon, transfer meat and vegetables to a serving platter; keep warm. Skim fat from pan juices. Stir together cornstarch and water. Add to juices. Cook and stir till thickened and bubbly, then cook and stir 2 minutes more. Spoon over meat and vegetables. Makes 6 servings.

Gingered Pork

The dark green leaves of bok choy provide a rich color contrast to the marinated pork, carrots, and water chestnuts.

1 **pound boneless pork**
⅓ **cup oyster sauce**
¼ **cup dry sherry**
2 **tablespoons water**
1 **teaspoon sugar**
¾ **cup cold water**
4 **teaspoons cornstarch**
1 **tablespoon cooking oil**
1 **tablespoon grated gingerroot**
2 **medium carrots, cut into julienne strips (⅔ cup)**
4 **cups sliced bok choy**
½ **of an 8-ounce can (½ cup) sliced water chestnuts, drained**
 Hot cooked rice

● Partially freeze pork; cut on the bias into thin bite-size strips. For marinade, stir together oyster sauce, sherry, the 2 tablespoons water, and sugar. Add pork, stirring to coat well. Cover and marinate at room temperature for 30 minutes or in the refrigerator for 2 hours, stirring occasionally. Drain pork, reserving marinade. Stir the ¾ cup cold water and cornstarch into reserved marinade. Set aside.

● Preheat a wok or large skillet over high heat; add cooking oil. (Add more oil as necessary during cooking.) Stir-fry gingerroot in hot oil for 15 seconds. Add carrots; stir-fry for 1 minute. Add bok choy; stir-fry about 3 minutes or till vegetables are crisp-tender. Remove from the wok.

● Add *half* of the pork to the hot wok. Stir-fry about 3 minutes or till no longer pink. Remove pork. Stir-fry remaining pork about 3 minutes. Return all pork to the wok. Stir in water chestnuts. Push from center of the wok.

● Stir marinade mixture; add to center of the wok. Cook and stir till thickened and bubbly. Cook and stir for 1 minute more. Return vegetables; stir ingredients together. Cook and stir for 1 minute. Serve immediately over rice. Makes 4 servings.

Slicing bok choy
For a distinct oriental touch and a sweet, mild flavor, add bok choy to your stir-fried dishes. To prepare bok choy, pull off one celerylike stalk, then thinly slice the white stem and dark green leaves into bite-size pieces. Repeat with additional stalks as needed.

Tabbouleh-Stuffed Whitefish

1 cup boiling water
½ cup bulgur
⅓ cup finely chopped seeded cucumber
¼ cup snipped parsley
1 green onion, sliced
1 tablespoon snipped fresh mint *or* 1 teaspoon dried mint, crushed
1 tablespoon lemon juice
1 tablespoon cooking oil
½ teaspoon salt
1 2- to 2½-pound scaled drawn whitefish, lake trout, *or* red snapper
Nonstick spray coating

● For stuffing, in a mixing bowl combine boiling water and bulgur. Let stand for 20 minutes. Drain well, then squeeze out excess water. Stir in cucumber, parsley, onion, mint, lemon juice, oil, and salt.

● To stuff fish, fill fish cavity with stuffing, lightly patting the stuffing to flatten evenly. (If all of the stuffing does not fit into fish, place remaining stuffing in a covered casserole and bake the last 25 minutes.) Tie or skewer fish closed.

● Spray a large shallow baking pan with nonstick coating. Place stuffed fish in the pan. Cover loosely with foil. Bake in a 350° oven about 40 minutes or till done. Makes 4 servings.

Swordfish and Fruit Kabobs

1 pound swordfish, sea bass, shark, *or* tuna steaks, cut 1 inch thick
¼ cup orange juice *and* 4 fresh plums, *or* one 15¼-ounce can pineapple chunks (juice pack)
2 tablespoons finely chopped onion
2 tablespoons dry sherry
2 tablespoons cooking oil
1 tablespoon sesame seed, toasted and crushed
1 clove garlic, minced
¼ teaspoon salt
⅛ teaspoon pepper
1 medium orange, cut into chunks
8 green onions, cut into 1½-inch pieces
Nonstick spray coating

● Remove skin and bones from fish. Cut fish into 1-inch pieces. Place in a plastic bag, then set bag in a bowl. If using pineapple, drain it, reserving ¼ cup juice. For marinade, combine orange juice or reserved pineapple juice, chopped onion, sherry, oil, sesame seed, garlic, salt, and pepper. Pour over fish. Close bag and refrigerate for 4 to 6 hours, turning bag occasionally.

● For kabobs, drain fish, reserving the marinade. If using plums, pit and cut them into quarters. Using 8 long skewers, alternately thread fish, plums or pineapple, orange chunks, and green onions, leaving about ¼ inch of space between pieces.

● Spray the *cold* rack of an unheated broiler pan with nonstick coating. Place kabobs on the rack. Brush with some marinade. Broil 4 inches from the heat for 5 minutes. Turn kabobs over. Brush with marinade. Broil about 4 minutes more or till fish is done. Brush with more marinade before serving. Serves 4.

To grill: Prepare Swordfish and Fruit Kabobs as above, *except* spray the *cold* grill rack with nonstick coating. Place kabobs on rack. Grill, uncovered, directly over *medium-hot* coals for 8 to 12 minutes or till done. Turn and brush often with marinade.

Swordfish and Fruit Kabobs

Ratatouille-Topped Fillets

1½ cups cubed peeled eggplant
2 medium tomatoes, seeded and chopped
1 8-ounce can reduced-sodium tomato sauce
1 small onion, thinly sliced and separated into rings
½ of a small zucchini, sliced ¼ inch thick (½ cup)
½ cup sliced fresh mushrooms
½ cup chopped green pepper
½ teaspoon dried basil, crushed
¼ teaspoon garlic powder
¼ teaspoon dried oregano, crushed
⅛ teaspoon salt
Nonstick spray coating
1 pound skinless flounder, haddock, orange roughy, *or* sole fillets

● For vegetable mixture, in a medium saucepan combine the eggplant, chopped tomatoes, tomato sauce, onion, zucchini, mushrooms, green pepper, basil, garlic powder, oregano, and salt. Bring the mixture to boiling, then reduce heat. Cover and simmer for 15 minutes. Uncover and simmer about 12 minutes more or till mixture is thickened.

● Meanwhile, spray a 12x7½x2-inch baking dish with non-stick coating. Measure thickness of fish. Sprinkle with *pepper*. If using large fillets, place them in a single layer in the baking dish, tucking under any thin edges. If using small fillets, stack them evenly in the baking dish.

● Spoon vegetable mixture over fish. Cover with foil. Bake in a 450° oven till fish is done (allow 6 to 8 minutes per ½-inch thickness). Transfer to a serving platter. Makes 4 servings.

Evenly cooking fillets
Fillets cook more evenly if you turn under any thin edges. This makes the fillets about the same thickness so that the thinner ends won't get done before the thicker ends.

If you're using small, thin fillets such as sole or flounder in the Ratatouille-Topped Fillets, you'll need to stack them so they'll all fit in the dish. But keep in mind that, for even cooking of the fish, the fillets should be stacked to about the same thickness.

Open-Face Vegewiches

The best use of tofu this side of the Orient!

    Nonstick spray coating
1 16-ounce package tofu
    (fresh bean curd), drained
4 1-ounce slices cheddar
    cheese, halved
1 medium onion, thinly sliced
    and separated into rings
1 cup sliced fresh mushrooms
½ cup thinly sliced carrot
½ cup thinly sliced celery
2 tablespoons water
1 tablespoon Worcestershire
    sauce
½ teaspoon cornstarch
8 ½-inch slices French bread,
    toasted

● Spray the rack of an unheated broiler pan with nonstick coating. Cut tofu into eight ½-inch slices, then place on the rack. Broil about 4 inches from the heat for 4 minutes. Turn and broil 1 to 2 minutes more or till light brown. Top each tofu slice with half of a cheese slice. Broil about 1 minute more or till cheese melts.

● Meanwhile, spray a saucepan with nonstick coating. Cook onion, mushrooms, carrot, and celery in the saucepan till tender. Combine water, Worcestershire sauce, and cornstarch; stir into vegetables. Cook and stir till thickened and bubbly, then cook and stir 1 minute more.

● To assemble sandwiches, place tofu on bread slices. Transfer to individual serving plates, then spoon vegetable mixture over sandwiches. Makes 4 servings.

Cheese and Spinach Casseroles

A cousin of quiche, with a cautious eye on cholesterol.

2 cups low-fat cottage cheese
3 egg whites
⅓ cup all-purpose flour
¾ teaspoon dried basil,
    crushed
⅛ teaspoon garlic powder
⅛ teaspoon pepper
8 ounces fresh spinach, torn
    (6 cups)
1 cup shredded mozzarella
    cheese (4 ounces)
1 8-ounce can water
    chestnuts, drained
    and chopped
    Nonstick spray coating
1 medium tomato, cut into
    8 thin slices

● In a blender container or food processor bowl combine cottage cheese and egg whites. Cover and blend till smooth. Stir together flour, basil, garlic powder, and pepper. Add cottage cheese mixture and mix well. Stir in spinach, *half* of the mozzarella cheese, and water chestnuts.

● Spray four au gratin dishes with nonstick coating. Spoon spinach mixture into the dishes, then place on a baking sheet. Cover loosely with foil. Bake in a 350° oven about 30 minutes or until a knife inserted near the center comes out clean. Arrange two tomato slices over each dish, then sprinkle with remaining mozzarella cheese. Bake about 3 minutes more or till cheese melts. Makes 4 servings.

Broccoli-Ham Soup

Prepare this elegant soup when unexpected guests arrive—it's ready in minutes.

¼ cup chopped onion
3 tablespoons butter *or* margarine
¼ cup all-purpose flour
1½ teaspoons instant chicken bouillon granules
1 teaspoon dry mustard
½ teaspoon dried thyme, crushed
⅛ teaspoon pepper
2 cups milk
2 cups water
2 cups broccoli flowerets *or* frozen cut broccoli
1½ cups cubed fully cooked ham

● In a 3-quart saucepan cook the chopped onion in butter or margarine till tender but not brown. Stir in flour, chicken bouillon granules, mustard, thyme, and pepper. Add milk and water all at once. Cook and stir over medium-high heat till thickened and bubbly.

● Stir fresh broccoli flowerets or frozen cut broccoli and cubed ham into saucepan. Return to boiling. Reduce heat; simmer for 4 to 6 minutes more or till the broccoli is tender and the soup is heated through, stirring occasionally. Makes 4 servings.

Curried Fish Soup

Serve a bowlful of this easy fish soup with a piece of crusty bread or an assortment of crackers.

1 16-ounce package frozen fish fillets
½ cup chopped onion
½ cup chopped celery
½ cup chopped carrot
2 teaspoons curry powder
2 tablespoons butter *or* margarine
2 14½-ounce cans chicken broth
1½ cups milk
4 teaspoons cornstarch

● Thaw fish at room temperature for 20 minutes. Cut the fish into ½-inch pieces; set aside.

● In a 3-quart saucepan cook the onion, celery, carrot, and curry powder in the butter or margarine till vegetables are tender but not brown.

● Stir in chicken broth all at once. Cook and stir about 5 minutes or till bubbly; stir in pieces of fish. Cook and stir for 4 to 5 minutes more or till fish flakes easily.

● Meanwhile, combine milk and cornstarch. Stir into fish mixture. Cook and stir till thickened and bubbly. Cook and stir 2 minutes more. Makes 6 servings.

Broccoli-Ham Soup

Cream of Potato Soup with Fish

Combine the new with the old. Add fish and nutmeg to an old-time favorite soup.

1½ cups cubed peeled potatoes
    (2 medium)
  1 cup water
  1 thinly sliced leek *or* ¼ cup
    chopped onion
  1 teaspoon instant chicken
    bouillon granules
    Dash white pepper
 12 ounces skinless flounder *or*
    orange roughy fillets
  1 13-ounce can (1⅔ cups)
    evaporated skim milk
 ⅛ teaspoon ground nutmeg

● In a medium saucepan combine the potatoes, water, leek or onion, bouillon granules, and pepper. Bring to boiling, then reduce heat. Cover and simmer for 10 minutes.

● Meanwhile, measure the thickness of the fish. Cut the fish into 1-inch pieces. Cover and refrigerate till needed.

● Transfer the cooked potato mixture to a blender container or food processor bowl. Cover and blend or process till smooth. Return to saucepan. Stir in milk and nutmeg. Add fish. Bring almost to boiling, then reduce heat. Cover and simmer gently till fish is done (allow about 2 minutes per ½-inch thickness of fish). *Do not boil.* Makes 4 servings.

German-Style Apple Stew

Serve with rye bread and you've got a hearty fall or winter supper.

1½ cups apple juice *or* apple
    cider
1½ cups water
  2 medium carrots, halved
    lengthwise, then cut into
    1½-inch pieces
  1 stalk celery, sliced
 ½ cup sliced green onion
  2 tablespoons cider vinegar
  2 teaspoons instant chicken
    bouillon granules
  1 teaspoon caraway seed
    Dash pepper
  1 pound skinless mahimahi *or*
    monkfish fillets (about 1
    inch thick)
 ¼ of a small head cabbage,
    finely shredded (about
    1¼ cups)
  1 apple, cored and thinly
    sliced

● In a large saucepan combine apple juice or apple cider, water, carrots, celery, onion, vinegar, bouillon granules, caraway seed, and pepper. Bring mixture to boiling, then reduce heat. Cover and simmer for 10 minutes.

● Meanwhile, cut fish into 1-inch pieces. Carefully add fish to juice mixture. Return just to boiling, then reduce heat. Cover and simmer gently for 2 minutes. Add the cabbage and apple. Return just to boiling, then reduce heat. Cover and simmer gently about 2 minutes more or till fish is done and vegetables are nearly tender. Makes 4 servings.

Minestrone

This traditional Italian soup is bursting with fresh vegetables, pasta, and beans.

2 stalks celery, chopped
1 large onion, chopped
1 clove garlic, minced
2 tablespoons olive oil *or*
    cooking oil
3 cups water
4 medium tomatoes, peeled
    and chopped, *or* one
    16-ounce can tomatoes,
    cut up
2 tablespoons snipped parsley
1 tablespoon instant beef
    bouillon granules
1 bay leaf
1½ teaspoons dried basil,
    crushed
½ teaspoon dried oregano,
    crushed
⅛ teaspoon pepper
1 cup sliced carrots
1 15-ounce can red kidney
    beans
1 9-ounce package frozen
    Italian green beans *or*
    cut green beans
2 ounces spaghetti, broken
    into 1-inch pieces (½ cup)
    Grated Parmesan cheese

● In a Dutch oven cook celery, onion, and garlic in hot oil till tender. Add water, fresh or *undrained* tomatoes, parsley, bouillon granules, bay leaf, basil, oregano, and pepper.

● Bring to boiling; reduce the heat. Cover and simmer for 30 minutes. Add carrots. Cover and simmer for 5 minutes more. Remove from the heat. Remove bay leaf. Stir in kidney beans, green beans, and spaghetti. Cool. Pour mixture into two 1-quart freezer containers. Seal, label, and freeze.

● **To serve,** transfer 1 portion of frozen mixture to a medium saucepan. Cover and cook over medium heat for 40 to 45 minutes or till heated through, stirring occasionally. Sprinkle each serving with cheese. Makes two 4-serving portions.

Classic Chef's Salad

You won't leave the table hungry after dining on one of these ample salads!

9 cups torn salad greens
6 ounces Swiss *or* cheddar cheese, cut into julienne strips
3 ounces fully cooked ham *or* cooked lean beef, cut into julienne strips
6 ounces cooked chicken *or* turkey, cut into julienne strips
¼ cup crumbled blue cheese, crumbled feta cheese, *or* grated Parmesan cheese (optional)
4 hard-cooked eggs, sliced
2 small green peppers, cut into strips
1 small cucumber, thinly sliced
1 cup cherry tomatoes, halved
¾ cup sliced radishes
¾ cup Creamy French Dressing

● Place the torn salad greens into 6 large individual salad bowls. Arrange Swiss or cheddar cheese strips, ham or beef strips, and chicken or turkey strips over salad greens; sprinkle with blue, feta, or Parmesan cheese, if desired.
● Add the hard-cooked egg slices, green pepper strips, cucumber slices, cherry tomato halves, and radishes. Serve salads with Creamy French Dressing. Makes 6 servings.

Creamy French Dressing: In a small mixer bowl combine 1 tablespoon *paprika*, 2 teaspoons *sugar*, 1 teaspoon *salt*, and dash ground *red pepper*. Add ¼ cup *vinegar* and 1 *egg*; beat well. Add 1 cup *salad oil* in a slow, steady stream, beating constantly with an electric mixer till thick. Cover; store remaining dressing in the refrigerator. Makes about 1⅔ cups.

Preparing Salad Greens

No matter what type of salad greens you buy, they should look fresh and perky. Storing greens in the refrigerator in a sealed plastic bag or crisper container will ensure crispness.

Several hours before using any greens, remove them from the refrigerator and wash them well under cold running water. Shake off any excess water and pat the greens dry with a kitchen towel or paper towel. Return them to the refrigerator to give them time to become crisp.

Tear, don't cut, the greens into bite-size pieces. Tearing exposes the juicy insides and allows dressing to be absorbed by the greens; cutting with a knife hastens darkening of the edges.

Grape and Pork Salad

The almonds add an extra crunch. Toast them in a 350° oven about 10 minutes or until they're light brown.

- 4 cups torn Bibb lettuce *or* Boston lettuce
- 2 cups torn romaine
- 2 cups seedless red grapes, halved
- 1½ cups cooked pork cut into julienne strips
- 3 tablespoons olive oil *or* salad oil
- 2 tablespoons water
- 2 tablespoons wine vinegar
- ¾ teaspoon ground coriander
- ½ teaspoon sugar
- ¼ teaspoon garlic salt
- ¼ cup slivered almonds, toasted

● In a very large mixing bowl combine the Bibb or Boston lettuce, romaine, grapes, and pork. Cover and chill while preparing the dressing.

● For dressing, in a screw-top jar combine olive oil or salad oil, water, vinegar, coriander, sugar, and garlic salt. Cover and shake well. Pour over lettuce mixture. Toss lightly to coat.

● To serve, spoon mixture onto 4 salad plates. Sprinkle with almonds. Makes 4 servings.

Tabbouleh with Lamb

Tabbouleh (tuh-BOO-luh) is a refreshing Middle Eastern salad featuring bulgur (a Turkish wheat). Chill the salad for several hours so the wheat soaks up the sensational mint dressing.

- 8 ounces cooked lamb *or* chicken
- ⅓ cup salad oil
- ⅓ cup lemon juice
- 2 tablespoons snipped fresh mint *or* 2 teaspoons dried mint, crushed
- ½ teaspoon salt
- ⅛ teaspoon pepper
- 2 cloves garlic, minced
- 2 cups boiling water
- 1 cup bulgur wheat
- ½ cup chopped celery
- ½ cup thinly sliced carrot
- ½ cup snipped parsley
- ¼ cup chopped green pepper
- ¼ cup sliced green onion
- 1¼ cups finely chopped cucumber
- 2 medium tomatoes, chopped
  Leaf lettuce

● If using lamb, trim any excess fat from it. Chop the lamb or chicken and place the meat in a large bowl. (You should have about 1½ cups.)

● For dressing, in a screw-top jar combine oil, lemon juice, mint, salt, pepper, and garlic. Cover and shake well. Pour dressing over meat. Let stand at room temperature for 30 minutes.

● Meanwhile, in a medium mixing bowl combine boiling water and bulgur. Let stand for 20 minutes. Drain well, then squeeze out excess water. Add bulgur, celery, carrot, parsley, green pepper, and onion to meat mixture. Toss lightly to coat. Cover and chill for 3 to 5 hours.

● To serve, stir in cucumber and tomatoes. Line 6 salad plates with lettuce leaves. Spoon bulgur mixture onto the plates. Makes 6 servings.

**Poultry-Filled
Summertime Melons**

Chicken and Fruit Toss

A fruit lover's delight—pineapple shells filled with pineapple, oranges, kiwi fruit, and lettuce, all tossed in a tangerine dressing.

¼ cup water
¼ cup frozen tangerine juice
    concentrate
1 tablespoon lemon juice *or*
    lime juice
1 teaspoon cornstarch
2 small pineapples, chilled
2 cups shredded iceberg
    lettuce
1½ cups cubed cooked chicken
1 orange, peeled and
    sectioned
1 kiwi fruit, peeled, sliced, and
    quartered
2 ounces Monterey Jack
    cheese, cut into 1-inch
    julienne sticks

● For dressing, in a small saucepan combine water, tangerine juice concentrate, lemon or lime juice, and cornstarch. Cook and stir till thickened and bubbly. Cook and stir for 2 minutes more. Remove from heat. Cover surface with waxed paper or clear plastic wrap. Cool slightly *without* stirring, then chill.

● Meanwhile, for pineapple shells use a sharp knife to cut the pineapples lengthwise in half, crown and all. Remove hard cores from pineapples. Cut out pineapple meat, leaving shells intact. Set pineapple shells aside.

● Cut pineapple meat into bite-size chunks. Set aside *3 cups* of the chunks. (Refrigerate remaining pineapple for another use.)

● In a medium mixing bowl combine reserved pineapple chunks, lettuce, chicken, orange sections, kiwi fruit, and cheese. Pour dressing over fruit mixture. Toss lightly to coat.

● Immediately spoon fruit mixture into pineapple shells. Place shells on 4 salad plates. Makes 4 servings.

Poultry-Filled Summertime Melons

Prefer honeydew melons? Use them in place of the cantaloupes.

½ cup pineapple yogurt
2 tablespoons mayonnaise *or*
    salad dressing
¼ teaspoon ground ginger
2 cups cubed cooked
    chicken *or* turkey
½ cup sliced celery
2 small cantaloupes
    Leaf lettuce
1 cup strawberries, halved
1 tablespoon sunflower nuts
    Whole strawberries
    (optional)

● For salad mixture, in a medium mixing bowl combine yogurt, mayonnaise or salad dressing, and ginger. Stir till well blended. Add chicken or turkey and celery. Toss lightly to coat. If desired, cover and chill for up to 8 hours.

● Meanwhile, cut cantaloupes lengthwise in half. Remove seeds. Using a melon-ball cutter, scoop the pulp out of the cantaloupes. Set aside and chill *2 cups* of the cantaloupe balls till serving time. (Refrigerate remaining balls for another use.)

● If desired, lay the shells on their sides. Using the melon-ball cutter, press down onto edges of shells, cutting scalloped edges.

● To serve, line 4 salad plates with lettuce leaves. Place the cantaloupe shells on the plates. Divide the reserved cantaloupe balls among the shells. Mound salad mixture in centers. Place strawberry halves around the salad mixtures. Sprinkle with sunflower nuts. If desired, garnish the plates with whole strawberries. Makes 4 servings.

Cabbage-Tuna Toss

When buying a head of cabbage, you can plan on one pound yielding about 5 cups of raw, coarsely shredded cabbage.

3 cups shredded cabbage
1 6½-ounce can tuna (water pack), drained and broken into chunks
¾ cup sliced fresh mushrooms
1 medium tomato, cut into thin wedges
½ of a medium cucumber, thinly sliced
12 pitted ripe olives, halved lengthwise
6 radishes, thinly sliced
⅓ cup mayonnaise *or* salad dressing
⅓ cup plain yogurt
2 teaspoons prepared mustard
¾ teaspoon dried dillweed

● For salad, in a large salad bowl combine shredded cabbage, tuna, mushrooms, tomato wedges, cucumber, ripe olives, and radishes. Cover salad; chill for several hours.

● For dressing, in a small bowl stir together mayonnaise or salad dressing, plain yogurt, prepared mustard, and dillweed. Cover; chill for several hours.

● Just before serving, pour dressing over salad; toss lightly to coat. Makes 4 servings.

Shredding cabbage

You can vary the size and texture of cabbage shreds simply by using different methods to cut the cabbage.

For long, coarse shreds, hold a quarter-head of cabbage firmly against a cutting surface; cut into even shreds with a long-bladed knife, as shown.

For shorter, medium shreds, push a quarter-head of cabbage across the coarse blade of a vegetable shredder.

For fine, juicy shreds, cut the cabbage into small wedges. Fill the blender about ½ full; cover with cold water. Cover and blend just till chopped; drain well.

Minted Pea-and-Fish Salad

To substitute a fresh herb for the dried form, use three times more of the fresh.

1 pound fresh *or* frozen fish
   fillets
¼ cup dry white wine
2 cups fresh peas *or* one
   10-ounce package frozen
   peas
1 teaspoon sugar
1 teaspoon dried mint,
   crushed
¼ teaspoon dried rosemary,
   crushed
½ cup mayonnaise *or* salad
   dressing
2 tablespoons lemon yogurt
2 tablespoons milk
   Several dashes bottled hot
   pepper sauce
½ cup thinly sliced celery
½ cup sliced fresh mushrooms
4 Bibb *or* Boston lettuce cups

● Thaw fish, if frozen. Cut into 1-inch cubes. Place fish in a large skillet. Add wine, ¼ cup *water,* and ¼ teaspoon *salt.* Bring to boiling, then reduce the heat. Cover and simmer for 3 to 6 minutes or till fish flakes easily with a fork. Drain. Cool fish slightly, then cover and chill.

● Meanwhile, in a small saucepan combine peas, sugar, mint, rosemary, ½ cup *water,* and ¼ teaspoon *salt.* Cover and cook till peas are nearly tender, adding more water if necessary (allow about 5 minutes for frozen or 10 to 12 minutes for fresh). Drain. Cool slightly, then cover and chill.

● For dressing, in a small bowl combine mayonnaise or salad dressing, yogurt, milk, and hot pepper sauce. Stir till well blended. Cover and chill.

● To serve, in a medium mixing bowl combine chilled fish, peas, celery, and mushrooms. Toss lightly to mix. Spoon pea mixture into lettuce cups. Drizzle with dressing. If desired, garnish with radish roses or tomato wedges. Makes 4 servings.

Salmon and Melon Salad

2 fresh *or* frozen salmon
   steaks, cut ¾ to 1 inch
   thick (about 1 pound
   total)
¾ cup water
1 tablespoon thinly sliced
   green onion
1 bay leaf
½ of a 5-ounce can (⅓ cup)
   evaporated milk
½ of a 6-ounce can (⅓ cup)
   frozen orange juice
   concentrate, thawed
3 teaspoons salad oil
½ of a medium cantaloupe,
   seeded
½ of a medium honeydew
   melon, seeded and peeled
2 cups torn Bibb lettuce *or*
   Boston lettuce
1½ cups seedless red grapes

● Thaw salmon, if frozen. In a skillet combine water, green onion, bay leaf, ¼ teaspoon *salt,* and dash *pepper.* Bring to boiling, then add salmon. Reduce heat. Cover and simmer for 5 to 10 minutes or till fish flakes easily with a fork. Drain and cool slightly. Remove skin and bones. Break salmon into large pieces. Cover and chill.

● For dressing, in a blender container combine evaporated milk and orange juice concentrate. Cover and blend about 5 seconds or till well combined. With lid ajar and blender on slow speed, *gradually* add oil, 1 teaspoon at a time. (When necessary, stop blender and scrape sides.) Cover and chill.

● Using a melon-ball cutter, scoop pulp out of the cantaloupe. Using a crinkle-edge cutter or a knife, cut the honeydew melon into ¾-inch cubes. (You should have about 1½ cups *each* of the cantaloupe balls and the honeydew melon cubes.)

● For salad, combine cantaloupe, honeydew melon, lettuce, and grapes. Pour dressing over mixture. Toss lightly. Add salmon and toss lightly again. Spoon mixture into 4 bowls. Serves 4.

Lemon Asparagus and Carrots

If you can't find the "baby" carrots, cut medium carrots into shorter lengths.

½ **pound asparagus** *or* **one 8-ounce package frozen asparagus spears**
½ **pound small carrots**
  Lemon juice
  Lemon pepper
  Lemon wedges (optional)
  Snipped parsley (optional)

● To prepare fresh asparagus, wash and scrape off scales. Snap off and discard the woody bases. Tie the whole asparagus spears in a bundle. Stand the bundle upright in a deep kettle, letting tips extend 2 to 3 inches above boiling salted water. Cover and cook for 10 to 15 minutes or till crisp-tender. (*Or,* cook frozen asparagus spears according to package directions.) Rinse the cooked asparagus spears in cold water; drain.

● Meanwhile, to prepare carrots, wash, trim, and peel the small carrots. Place the carrots in a steamer basket above boiling water. Cover and steam about 15 minutes or till crisp-tender. Rinse the cooked carrots in cold water; drain.

● Cover and chill the cooked and drained asparagus spears and carrots. To serve, arrange the asparagus spears and carrots on a serving platter. Sprinkle with a little lemon juice and lemon pepper. Garnish with lemon wedges and parsley, if desired. Makes 6 servings.

Buying and Storing Fresh Asparagus

You'll be able to find fresh asparagus in most markets from mid-February through June. Choose firm, straight stalks with tight, compact tips. Asparagus with wilted stalks or loose tips may be tough and rather stringy.

Wrap the stem ends of the asparagus in moist paper towels before refrigerating in a plastic bag or covered container. Use fresh asparagus within two days.

1 Cooking fresh asparagus spears

Begin preparing asparagus spears by rinsing them and gently scraping off the scales with a knife. Remove the woody bases by breaking stalks instead of cutting them. Stalks will snap easily where tender part begins.

Tie the asparagus stalks together in a bundle. Stand the bundle upright in a deep kettle of boiling salted water. Let tips extend 2 to 3 inches above boiling water to avoid overcooking. (*Or,* cook in a saucepan in a small amount of boiling salted water with tips propped up out of the water with crumpled foil.) Cover and cook for 10 to 15 minutes or till crisp-tender.

2 Steaming carrots

Before steaming, wash, trim, and peel the small carrots. (*Or,* if you need to use medium carrots, cut them into 3- to 4-inch lengths.)

Place the carrots in a steamer basket. The steamer basket will allow the carrots to steam without coming in contact with the boiling liquid.

Place the basket of carrots over (but not touching) boiling water in a saucepan. Cover the pan and steam the carrots about 15 minutes or till crisp-tender.

Duchess Potatoes

If you don't have a pastry bag and tip for piping the potatoes, just spoon them into mounds.

1½ cups cooked and mashed
  potatoes
1 to 2 tablespoons light cream
  or milk
2 tablespoons butter *or*
  margarine
1 egg
¼ teaspoon salt
  Several dashes ground
  nutmeg
  Dash pepper
2 tablespoons butter *or*
  margarine, melted

● In a large mixing bowl or a small mixer bowl, combine warm potatoes, cream or milk, 2 tablespoons butter or margarine, egg, salt, nutmeg, and pepper. Mash with a potato masher or beat with an electric mixer on low speed till smooth.

● Line a baking sheet with waxed paper. Using a pastry bag with a large star tip, pipe potato mixture into 6 mounds onto baking sheet. Freeze about 45 minutes or till firm. Remove potato mounds from baking sheet and transfer to a freezer container or bag. Seal, label, and freeze.

● **To serve,** place frozen potato mounds on a greased baking sheet. Brush with 2 tablespoons melted butter or margarine. Bake, uncovered, in a 375° oven for 20 to 25 minutes or till heated through. Makes 6 servings.

Piping the potatoes
Carefully spoon the potato mixture into a pastry bag fitted with a large open-star writing tip. Fold the bag and hold it closed with your writing hand. Support the filled pastry bag with your other hand.

To pipe the mixture, hold the filled bag perpendicular to the baking sheet. Then force the potato mixture through the tip by squeezing the end of the bag with your writing hand.

Italian-Style Eggplant Slices

A crisp, bread crumb coating complements the soft texture of the baked eggplant.

1   small eggplant, cut into
    ½-inch slices (about 12
    ounces)
½ cup creamy Italian *or*
    creamy cucumber salad
    dressing
¾ cup fine dry bread crumbs
1   large tomato, very thinly
    sliced
⅓ cup shredded mozzarella *or*
    Monterey Jack cheese

● Dip eggplant slices into creamy Italian or creamy cucumber salad dressing, then into bread crumbs to coat.
● Place the eggplant slices in an ungreased 15x10x1-inch baking pan. Bake in a 350° oven for 25 to 30 minutes or till eggplant is tender.
● Top *each* eggplant slice with a thin tomato slice and shredded mozzarella or Monterey Jack cheese. Bake about 2 minutes more or till cheese melts. Makes 5 servings.

Chilled Sesame Broccoli

Look for sesame oil, with its concentrated nutlike flavor, in supermarkets or Oriental food shops.

1   pound broccoli, cut into
    spears, *or* one 10-ounce
    package frozen broccoli
    spears
2   tablespoons vinegar
1   tablespoon soy sauce
1   teaspoon sugar
¼ teaspoon sesame oil
1   tablespoon sesame seed,
    toasted

● If using fresh broccoli, cut off broccoli flowerets; set aside. Bias-slice the broccoli stems into ½-inch-thick pieces. Cook stems, covered, in 1 inch of boiling salted water for 5 minutes; add reserved broccoli flowerets. Cook about 5 minutes more or till crisp-tender. Drain well. (Or, if using frozen broccoli cook spears according to package directions, *except* cook for only *half* of the suggested time. Drain the cooked broccoli. Cut off flowerets; bias-slice stems into ½-inch-thick pieces.) Cover and chill cooked broccoli.
● In a screw-top jar combine vinegar, soy sauce, sugar, and sesame oil. Cover and shake well to mix.
● Shake vinegar mixture again just before serving. Drizzle over chilled broccoli; toss gently. Sprinkle with toasted sesame seed. Makes 4 servings.

Herbed Fresh Tomato Soup

For robust flavor, make this side-dish soup when tomatoes are at their peak. Then freeze portions of the soup to enjoy at your convenience.

2 medium onions, thinly
   sliced
2 tablespoons olive oil *or*
   cooking oil
2½ cups water
6 medium tomatoes, peeled
   and quartered (about 2
   pounds)
1 6-ounce can tomato paste
2 tablespoons snipped fresh
   basil *or* 2 teaspoons dried
   basil, crushed
1 tablespoon snipped fresh
   thyme *or* 1 teaspoon dried
   thyme, crushed
1 tablespoon instant chicken
   bouillon granules
½ teaspoon sugar
½ teaspoon salt
¼ teaspoon pepper
   Few dashes bottled hot
    pepper sauce
   Snipped parsley

● In a large saucepan cook onion in hot oil till tender. Stir in water, tomatoes, tomato paste, basil, thyme, bouillon granules, sugar, salt, pepper, and hot pepper sauce. Bring to boiling; reduce the heat. Cover and simmer for 40 minutes.

● Place about one-third of the tomato mixture in a blender container or food processor bowl; cover and blend till smooth. (Or press mixture through a food mill.) Repeat with remaining mixture; cool. Pour mixture into two 3-cup freezer containers. Seal, label, and freeze.

● **To serve,** transfer 1 portion of the frozen mixture to a medium saucepan. Cover and cook over medium heat for 20 to 25 minutes or till heated through, stirring occasionally. Sprinkle with parsley before serving. Makes two 4-serving portions.

French Onion Soup

You can toast the bread slices in your broiler for 1 to 1½ minutes per side.

3 large onions, thinly sliced
1 clove garlic, minced
¼ cup butter *or* margarine
3 10½-ounce cans condensed beef broth
2 cups water
6 1-inch slices French bread
6 1-ounce slices Swiss *or* Gruyère cheese
  Grated Parmesan cheese

● In a large saucepan cook onion and garlic in butter or margarine, covered, over low heat about 20 minutes or till very tender. Stir occasionally; remove from heat. Stir in beef broth and water. Pour into a 2-quart freezer container. Seal, label, and freeze.

● **To serve,** transfer frozen mixture to a large saucepan. Cover and cook over medium heat about 25 minutes or till heated through, stirring occasionally.

● Meanwhile, toast bread slices; arrange on a baking sheet. Top bread with Swiss or Gruyère cheese. Sprinkle lightly with Parmesan cheese. Broil 3 to 4 inches from the heat for 2 to 3 minutes or till cheese is light brown and bubbly. Ladle hot soup into serving bowls. Top with bread slices. Makes 6 servings.

Broiling the bread and cheese

While the frozen soup is reheating, toast the slices of French bread. Just before serving, top each bread slice with a slice of cheese. Sprinkle lightly with the Parmesan cheese.

Broil the bread slices 3 to 4 inches from the heat for 2 to 3 minutes or till the cheese is light brown and bubbly. With a spatula, transfer one slice of bread to each individual bowl of soup.

Mustard-Sauced Medley

Dijon-style mustard is based on a mustard made in Dijon, France. Its tart, yet pleasing flavor complements the broccoli, carrots, and onion in this stir-fried side dish.

⅓ cup milk
2 teaspoons Dijon-style mustard
1½ teaspoons cornstarch
1 teaspoon instant chicken bouillon granules
1 tablespoon cooking oil
2 medium carrots, thinly bias sliced (1 cup)
¾ pound fresh broccoli, cut up (3 cups) (see tip, page 30)
1 medium onion, thinly sliced and separated into rings

● For sauce, stir together milk, mustard, cornstarch, and bouillon granules. Set aside.
● Preheat a wok or large skillet over high heat; add cooking oil. (Add more oil as necessary during cooking.) Stir-fry carrots in hot oil for 1 minute. Add broccoli and onion; stir-fry about 4 minutes or till vegetables are crisp-tender. Push vegetables from center of the wok.
● Stir sauce; add to center of the wok or skillet. Cook and stir till thickened and bubbly. Cook and stir for 1 minute more. Stir in stir-fried vegetables to coat with the sauce. Serve immediately. Makes 6 servings.

Zucchini and Tomato Parmesan

Popular Italian ingredients, including garlic and Parmesan cheese, make this stir-fried recipe as flavorful as it is colorful. (Also pictured on the cover.)

1 tablespoon cooking oil
1 clove garlic, minced
2 medium zucchini, halved lengthwise and sliced ¼-inch thick (2½ cups)
4 green onions, bias-sliced into 1-inch lengths (¾ cup)
2 medium tomatoes, seeded and chopped (1 cup)
¼ cup snipped parsley
½ cup grated Parmesan *or* Romano cheese

● Preheat a wok or large skillet over high heat; add cooking oil. (Add more oil as necessary during cooking.) Stir-fry garlic in hot oil for 15 seconds. Add zucchini; stir-fry for 1½ minutes. Add green onions; stir-fry about 1½ minutes or till vegetables are crisp-tender.
● Stir in tomatoes and parsley. Cover and cook about 1 minute or till heated through. Sprinkle with Parmesan or Romano cheese; toss gently. Serve immediately. Makes 6 servings.

Zucchini and Tomato Parmesan

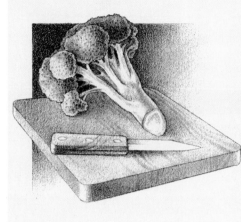

Preparing Broccoli for Stir-Frying

Broccoli grows year-round, but the supply is less plentiful during the hot summer months. Look for firm, tender stalks bearing small, crisp leaves. The dark green or purplish-green flowerets should be tightly closed, showing no signs of flowering.

To prepare broccoli for stir-frying, cut the flowerets into bite-size pieces and thinly slice or bias-slice the stems. When broccoli isn't quite at its peak, use a sharp knife to peel the tough outer portion of the stems to make the broccoli more tender.

Broccoli with Shallots

Mild-flavored shallots look like miniature dried onions with reddish-brown skins.

2 tablespoons butter *or* margarine, melted
1 tablespoon lemon juice
¼ teaspoon dried rosemary, crushed
1 tablespoon cooking oil
¾ pound fresh broccoli, cut up (3 cups) (see tip, above)
1 medium sweet red *or* green pepper, cut into ¾-inch pieces (¾ cup)
2 tablespoons chopped shallot *or* sliced green onion

● For butter sauce, stir together melted butter or margarine, lemon juice, and rosemary. Set aside.
● Preheat a wok or large skillet over high heat; add cooking oil. (Add more oil as necessary during cooking.) Stir-fry broccoli in hot oil for 2 minutes. Add sweet red or green pepper pieces and shallot or green onion; stir-fry about 2 minutes or till vegetables are crisp-tender.
● Pour butter sauce over vegetables. Toss gently till vegetables are well coated. Serve immediately. Makes 4 servings.

Orange-Walnut Cauliflower and Carrots

In testing our recipes containing walnuts or pecans, we found that the color of a dish looked best when the nuts were stirred in at the very end of stir-frying.

3 medium carrots, roll cut
    (1 cup)
⅓ cup orange juice
1 teaspoon cornstarch
1 teaspoon brown sugar
1 tablespoon cooking oil
1½ cups thinly sliced
    cauliflower
¼ cup chopped walnuts

● Cook carrots, covered, in a small amount of boiling salted water for 3½ minutes; drain. For sauce, stir together orange juice, cornstarch, and brown sugar. Set aside.

● Preheat a wok or large skillet over high heat; add cooking oil. (Add more oil as necessary during cooking.) Stir-fry cauliflower in hot oil for 2½ minutes. Add carrots; stir-fry about 2½ minutes or till vegetables are crisp-tender. Push vegetables from center of the wok.

● Stir sauce; add to center of the wok or skillet. Cook and stir till thickened and bubbly. Cook and stir for 1 minute more. Stir in vegetables and walnuts to coat with sauce. Serve immediately. Makes 4 servings.

Oriental Pea Pods

Grated fresh gingerroot will add a distinct aromatic, fresh quality to your stir-fries. If you prefer to use ground ginger in this recipe, use ¼ teaspoon.

⅓ cup cold water
2 tablespoons soy sauce
2 teaspoons cornstarch
1 teaspoon sugar
½ teaspoon grated gingerroot
⅛ teaspoon freshly ground
    pepper
1 tablespoon cooking oil
2 medium carrots, thinly bias
    sliced (1 cup)
1 cup fresh pea pods *or* ½ of a
    6-ounce package frozen
    pea pods, thawed
5 green onions, bias-sliced
    into 1-inch lengths (1 cup)
½ cup sliced fresh mushrooms
1 8-ounce can sliced water
    chestnuts, drained

● For sauce, stir together water, soy sauce, cornstarch, sugar, gingerroot, and pepper. Set aside.

● Preheat a wok or large skillet over high heat; add cooking oil. (Add more oil as necessary during cooking.) Stir-fry carrots in hot oil for 2 minutes. Add pea pods; stir-fry for 30 seconds. Add onions and mushrooms; stir-fry about 1½ minutes or till vegetables are crisp-tender. Stir in water chestnuts. Push vegetables from center of the wok.

● Stir sauce; add to center of the wok or skillet. Cook and stir till thickened and bubbly. Cook and stir for 1 minute more. Stir in the vegetables to coat with the sauce. Serve immediately. Makes 4 servings.

Pasta 'n' Tomatoes

Stuffed to the brim with cheesy pasta!

1   cup tiny bow tie pasta
        (tripolini)
4   large fresh tomatoes
        (about 8 ounces each)
¼   cup sliced green onion
1   clove garlic, minced
1   tablespoon snipped fresh
        basil *or* 1 teaspoon dried
        basil, crushed
1   tablespoon butter *or*
        margarine
1   3-ounce package cream
        cheese, cubed
¼   cup shredded mozzarella,
        cheddar, *or* Swiss cheese
        (1 ounce)
¼   cup grated Parmesan cheese
⅛   teaspoon pepper
⅓   cup cubed fully cooked ham
¼   cup milk

● Cook pasta conventionally according to the package directions. Drain and keep warm. Meanwhile, cut a thin slice off the stem end of the tomatoes. Hollow out the tomatoes, leaving a ¼- to ½-inch-thick shell. Discard seeds. Chop the tomato insides and tops; set aside.

● In a 2-cup measure combine onion, garlic, basil, and butter or margarine. Cover with vented clear plastic wrap. Cook on 100% power (high) for 1 to 2 minutes or till the onion is tender. Stir together the warm pasta; cream cheese; mozzarella, cheddar, or Swiss cheese; Parmesan cheese; and pepper. Stir till the cheeses are slightly melted. Stir in the onion mixture, ham, and milk.

● Spoon about *½ cup* of the pasta mixture into *each* tomato. Spoon the remaining pasta mixture into an 8x8x2-inch baking dish. Sprinkle with the chopped tomato. Arrange the filled tomatoes in the dish atop the pasta mixture. Cover with vented clear plastic wrap. Cook on high for 6 to 8 minutes or till heated through. Let stand, covered, for 1 minute. Makes 4 servings.

Cheese-Filled Zucchini

Give this a try—hollow out zucchini with a melon baller.

2   4- to 6-inch zucchini, halved
        lengthwise
2   tablespoons water
¼   cup chopped onion
1   clove garlic, minced
1   slightly beaten egg
¾   cup shredded Monterey
        Jack cheese (3 ounces)
½   cup corn bread stuffing mix
1   tablespoon butter *or*
        margarine, melted
1   tablespoon grated
        Parmesan cheese

● Scoop out the pulp of the zucchini halves, leaving a ¼-inch-thick shell. Chop the zucchini pulp; set aside. Place zucchini shells, cut side down, in an 8x8x2-inch baking dish. Add the water. Cover with vented clear plastic wrap. Cook on 100% power (high) for 2 to 4 minutes or till crisp-tender. Drain. Place, cut side up, in the 8x8x2-inch baking dish.

● In a 1-quart casserole combine the chopped pulp, onion, and garlic. Cook, covered, on high for 3 to 5 minutes or till tender. Drain in a colander, pressing out the excess liquid. In the 1-quart casserole stir together the egg, Monterey Jack cheese, stuffing mix, and butter or margarine. Stir in the zucchini pulp mixture. Spoon into the cooked zucchini shells. Sprinkle with Parmesan cheese. Cover with vented clear plastic wrap. Cook on high for 3 to 5 minutes or till the filling is heated through, rearranging once. Makes 4 servings.

Pasta 'n' Tomatoes

Cumin Peppers and Onion

If you can't find a sweet red pepper, substitute a sweet yellow or green pepper.

½ of a medium green pepper, cut into strips
½ of a medium sweet red pepper, cut into strips
1 small onion, sliced and separated into rings
1 tablespoon butter *or* margarine
⅛ teaspoon ground cumin

● In a 1-quart casserole combine green pepper strips, red pepper strips, onion, butter or margarine, and cumin. Cook, covered, on 100% power (high) for 3 to 5 minutes or till the vegetables are crisp-tender, stirring once. Serve with beef, pork, lamb, or poultry. Makes 3 servings.

Peas and Walnuts

2 cups shelled peas *or* one 10-ounce package frozen peas
¼ cup chopped onion
1 tablespoon butter *or* margarine
1 teaspoon lemon juice
½ teaspoon dried dillweed
⅛ teaspoon salt
Dash pepper
¼ cup broken walnuts, toasted

● If using fresh peas, in a 1-quart casserole combine peas, onion, and 2 tablespoons *water*. Cook, covered, on 100% power (high) for 6 to 8 minutes or till peas are tender, stirring once. If using frozen peas, cook peas and onion according to the pea package microwave directions. Let the pea mixture stand, covered, while preparing the dill butter.

● For dill butter, in a 1-cup measure combine butter or margarine, lemon juice, dillweed, salt, and pepper. Cook, uncovered, on high for 30 to 40 seconds or till butter is melted. Drain the pea mixture. Toss the pea mixture with the dill butter and walnuts. Makes 4 servings.

Parmesan-Topped Tomato Slices

Richly topped with sour cream, mayonnaise, and Parmesan cheese.

2 large *or* 3 medium tomatoes, sliced ½ inch thick
¼ cup dairy sour cream
¼ cup mayonnaise *or* salad dressing
1 teaspoon lemon juice
¼ cup grated Parmesan cheese

● Place tomato slices in an 8x8x2-inch baking dish, overlapping slices slightly, if necessary. Stir together sour cream, mayonnaise or salad dressing, and lemon juice. Dollop atop tomato slices. Sprinkle with Parmesan cheese. Cook, uncovered, on 100% power (high) for 2½ to 4½ minutes or till heated through. Makes 4 servings.

Spicy Squash Bake

Check your grocer's Mexican section for bottled salsa.

1 pound of a banana squash
  or butternut squash,
  peeled and cut into
  ¾-inch cubes
2 tablespoons water
¼ cup finely chopped onion
1 clove garlic, minced
1 tablespoon butter *or*
  margarine
½ cup salsa
½ cup shredded cheddar
  cheese (2 ounces)
⅛ teaspoon pepper

● In a 1½-quart casserole combine the squash cubes and water. Cook, covered, on 100% power (high) for 6 to 8 minutes or till tender, stirring once. Drain. In the 1-quart casserole cook the onion and garlic in butter or margarine, uncovered, on high for 1 to 2 minutes or till the onion is tender.

● Stir the salsa, *half* of the cheese, and the pepper into the onion mixture. Gently fold in the squash. Cook, uncovered, on high for 2 to 3 minutes or till heated through. Top with the remaining cheese. Let stand, covered, for 1 to 2 minutes or till cheese is melted. Makes 4 servings.

Harvest Vegetable Bake

You can get these fresh vegetables during the fall and winter.

1 cup shredded carrot
½ cup shredded rutabaga
¼ cup shredded sweet potato
2 tablespoons chopped onion
1 tablespoon water
1½ cups cooked rice
¾ cup shredded Monterey
  Jack cheese (3 ounces)
¼ cup milk
¼ teaspoon salt
¼ teaspoon lemon pepper
  Dash ground nutmeg
¼ cup shredded Monterey
  Jack cheese (1 ounce)
  Green onion (optional)

● In a 1-quart casserole combine carrot, rutabaga, sweet potato, onion, and water. Cook, covered, on 100% power (high) for 2 to 4 minutes or just till vegetables are tender, stirring once.

● Stir in cooked rice, ¾ cup cheese, milk, salt, lemon pepper, and nutmeg. Cook, uncovered, on high for 4 to 6 minutes or till heated through, stirring once. Sprinkle the ¼ cup cheese atop. Let stand, covered, for 2 to 3 minutes or till the cheese is melted. Garnish with green onion, if desired. Makes 4 servings.

Fruit Slaw

Orange yogurt replaces the traditional mayonnaise-style dressing usually found on slaw.

3 **cups shredded cabbage**
1 **orange, peeled and sectioned**
1 **cup halved seedless red grapes**
½ **cup sliced celery**
1 **8-ounce carton orange yogurt**
1 **small apple, cored and chopped**
¼ **cup sunflower nuts (optional)**
Cabbage leaves

● In a large salad bowl combine shredded cabbage, orange sections, halved red grapes, and sliced celery.
● For dressing, combine the orange yogurt and chopped apple. Spread dressing over cabbage mixture. Cover; chill.
● Just before serving, gently toss salad; sprinkle with sunflower nuts, if desired. Serve on cabbage-lined plates. Makes 10 servings.

Spinach-Orange Toss

The piquant flavor of the blue cheese adds zip to this lightly flavored salad.

4 **cups torn fresh spinach, lettuce, *or* romaine**
½ **teaspoon finely shredded orange peel (set aside)**
2 **oranges, peeled and sectioned**
¾ **cup sliced fresh mushrooms**
⅓ **cup crumbled blue cheese**
3 **tablespoons salad oil**
1 **tablespoon lemon juice**
¼ **teaspoon grated gingerroot**
¼ **cup slivered almonds, toasted**

● For salad, in a large salad bowl place torn spinach, lettuce, or romaine. Add orange sections, sliced fresh mushrooms, and crumbled blue cheese. Toss lightly.
● For dressing, in a screw-top jar combine salad oil, lemon juice, gingerroot, and orange peel. Cover and shake well to mix.
● Pour dressing over salad. Toss lightly to coat. Sprinkle toasted almonds over salad. Serve immediately. Makes 6 servings.

Fruit Slaw

Citrus-Marinated Salad

If you score the peel of the cucumber by running the tines of a fork down the peel before slicing, you'll get attractive slices that are tender to eat.

2 oranges
1 grapefruit
1 avocado, seeded, peeled, and sliced
½ of a small cucumber, scored and thinly sliced
½ of a small onion, thinly sliced and separated into rings
    Orange juice
¼ cup wine vinegar
1 tablespoon sugar
    Dash salt
    Dash pepper
    Lettuce leaves

● Peel the oranges and the grapefruit. Section the oranges and the grapefruit over a small bowl so you catch the fruit juices; reserve juices.

● In a large bowl combine the orange and grapefruit sections, avocado slices, cucumber slices, and onion rings; set aside.

● For the marinade, measure the reserved fruit juices; add enough orange juice to make ⅓ cup. Combine the juice mixture, vinegar, sugar, salt, and pepper. Pour over fruit mixture; toss gently. Cover and marinate in the refrigerator for several hours, stirring occasionally.

● Before serving, use a slotted spoon to remove fruit mixture from marinade. Arrange fruit mixture on lettuce-lined plates. Drizzle marinade over each salad. Makes 4 servings.

Sunflower-Strawberry Salad

Try strawberry, peach, or another flavor of yogurt to vary the taste slightly.

1 medium apple, cored and chopped
1 cup halved seedless green grapes
1 cup sliced strawberries
½ cup sliced celery
¼ cup raisins
½ cup lemon yogurt
2 tablespoons sunflower nuts
    Lettuce leaves

● In a bowl combine chopped apple, halved grapes, sliced strawberries, sliced celery, and raisins; toss gently. Fold in the lemon yogurt. Cover and chill.

● Just before serving, stir in sunflower nuts. Serve on lettuce-lined plates. Makes 6 servings.

New Potatoes Dijon

New potatoes are small, immature potatoes and not a specific variety.

1 **pound tiny new potatoes** *or* **medium potatoes**
¼ **cup tarragon vinegar** *or* **vinegar**
3 **tablespoons olive** *or* **cooking oil**
1 **tablespoon Dijon-style mustard**
¼ **teaspoon salt**
¼ **teaspoon dried basil, crushed**
⅛ **teaspoon pepper**
1 **cup torn fresh spinach**

● Scrub the potatoes. Remove a narrow strip of peel from the center of each new potato or quarter each medium potato.

● Cook potatoes, covered, in boiling salted water till tender (allow 10 to 15 minutes for new potatoes; 20 to 25 minutes for quartered medium potatoes). Drain well.

● For dressing, in a screw-top jar combine vinegar, olive or cooking oil, mustard, salt, dried basil, and pepper. Cover and shake well to mix. Pour dressing over the cooked and drained potatoes. Cover potato mixture; chill for several hours, stirring occasionally.

● To serve, add torn fresh spinach to potato mixture. Toss lightly. Serve immediately. Makes 6 servings.

Sectioning Citrus Fruits

To section grapefruit or oranges, begin by cutting off the peel and the white membrane. Work on a cutting board and cut down from the top of the fruit. (If desired, first cut a thin slice from one end of the fruit so it will sit level on the cutting board.) You'll need a sharp utility knife or a serrated knife for peeling citrus fruits.

Next, remove the sections by cutting into the center of the fruit between one section and the membrane. Then turn the knife and slide the knife down the other side of the section next to the membrane. Remove any seeds.

Pasta Spinach Salad

Pasta Spinach Salad

Don't travel to Athens for feta cheese—it's right in your grocer's dairy case.

6 ounces rigatoni *or* cavatelli
2 medium tomatoes, peeled, seeded, and chopped
½ cup crumbled feta cheese (2 ounces)
⅓ cup low-calorie Italian salad dressing
¼ cup sliced green onion
2 tablespoons sliced pitted ripe olives
6 cups torn fresh spinach

● Cook pasta according to package directions, then drain. In a bowl combine pasta, tomatoes, cheese, salad dressing, green onion, and olives. Toss gently to coat. Cover and chill. Arrange spinach on a serving platter; spoon on pasta. Makes 8 servings.

Layered Vegetable Salad

A make-ahead marvel that's great for a large gathering.

1 medium head lettuce, torn into pieces (6 cups)
1 10-ounce package frozen peas, thawed
2 cups thinly sliced cauliflower flowerets
1 cup shredded carrot
2 cups cherry tomatoes, halved
1 cup shredded mozzarella cheese (4 ounces)
½ cup plain low-fat yogurt
⅓ cup reduced-calorie mayonnaise
2 tablespoons sliced green onion
Paprika

● In a large glass bowl layer *half* of the torn lettuce, the peas, cauliflower, and carrot. Add remaining lettuce and tomato halves; sprinkle with cheese. Stir together yogurt and mayonnaise, then spread over top of salad. Cover and chill several hours or overnight. Sprinkle with green onion and paprika. Toss before serving. Makes 12 servings.

Cantaloupe Sorbet

Sorbet (SOR-but) is French for sherbet. (Pictured on page 44.)

1 cup orange juice
¼ cup sugar
2 cups chopped cantaloupe
½ cup light cream
3 tablespoons lemon juice
2 egg whites
¼ cup sugar
   Cantaloupe halves, chilled
   (optional)

● In a saucepan combine orange juice and ¼ cup sugar; bring to boiling, stirring occasionally to dissolve sugar. Reduce heat; simmer for 5 minutes. Cool.

● In a blender container or food processor bowl combine 2 cups chopped cantaloupe and light cream. Cover; blend or process about 1 minute or till smooth. Stir in the lemon juice and the cooled orange juice mixture. Transfer mixture to a 12x7½x2-inch baking dish or a 9x9x2-inch baking pan. Cover; freeze about 4 hours or till firm.

● Beat egg whites with an electric mixer on medium speed till soft peaks form (tips curl). Gradually add ¼ cup sugar, beating till stiff peaks form (tips stand straight). Break the frozen mixture into chunks; transfer mixture to a chilled mixer bowl. Beat frozen mixture with the electric mixer till smooth, but not melted. Fold in the beaten egg whites. Return to the 12x7½x2-inch baking dish. Cover; freeze sorbet for several hours or till firm.

● Let sorbet stand at room temperature about 5 minutes before serving. Serve sorbet on chilled cantaloupe halves, if desired. Makes 6 servings.

Honeydew Melon Sorbet: Prepare Cantaloupe Sorbet as above, *except* substitute chopped *honeydew melon* for the chopped cantaloupe. Stir in a few drops *green food coloring* with the lemon juice and cooled orange juice mixture, if desired. Serve on chilled *honeydew melon wedges,* if desired.

Watermelon Sorbet: Prepare Cantaloupe Sorbet as above, *except* substitute chopped *watermelon* for the chopped cantaloupe. Stir in a few drops *red food coloring* with the lemon juice and cooled orange juice mixture, if desired. Serve on chilled *watermelon slices,* if desired.

1 Beating a sorbet

After blending and freezing the fruit mixture, remove it from the freezer. Use a plastic or wooden spoon to break the mixture into chunks. The chunks should be small enough for easy mixing with an electric mixer.

Transfer the broken-up mixture to a large, chilled mixer bowl.

2

Begin beating the frozen chunks with an electric mixer on low speed. When the large chunks are broken up, continue beating with the electric mixer on high speed.

Beat till smooth, but do not allow the mixture to melt. Scrape down the sides of the bowl as necessary.

Fold in the beaten egg whites. The egg whites give the sorbet its fluffy and light texture.

Before serving, let the sorbet stand at room temperature about 5 minutes for easier scooping with an ice cream scoop.

Watermelon Sorbet
(see recipe, page 42)

Cantaloupe Sorbet
(see recipe, page 42)

Honeydew Melon Sorbet
(see recipe, page 42)

Apples Poached in Sherry

The best cooking apples are firm varieties such as Rome Beauty, Granny Smith, and Jonathan.

4 medium cooking apples
⅔ cup apple juice *or* apple
    cider
¼ cup raisins
¼ cup dry sherry
3 inches stick cinnamon
1 teaspoon finely shredded
    lemon peel

● Core the apples. Peel off a strip around the top of each apple.
● In a medium skillet combine the apple juice or apple cider, raisins, dry sherry, stick cinnamon, and lemon peel.
● Bring sherry mixture to boiling. Add the apples to the skillet. Reduce heat; cover and simmer for 10 minutes, spooning the sherry mixture over apples occasionally. Turn apples over; cover and simmer for 3 to 5 minutes more or till tender. Remove the stick cinnamon.
● Serve apples warm. Spoon poaching liquid over apples, if desired. Makes 4 servings.

Fruity Floating Islands

For the freshest-tasting and best-looking poached meringues, serve your guests these delicacies the same day you make them.

3 egg whites
¼ teaspoon cream of tartar
¼ cup sugar
1¼ cups milk
3 slightly beaten egg yolks
2 tablespoons sugar
    Milk
½ teaspoon vanilla
    Dash ground nutmeg
    (optional)
3 cups desired fresh fruit*

● For meringue, beat egg whites and cream of tartar with an electric mixer on medium speed till soft peaks form (tips curl). Gradually add the ¼ cup sugar, beating till stiff peaks form (tips stand straight).
● In a heavy 10-inch skillet heat the 1¼ cups milk till hot but *not bubbling*. Drop meringue by spoonfuls into milk, making 6 mounds. Simmer, uncovered, about 5 minutes or till meringues are set. Lift meringues from milk with a slotted spoon. Drain meringues on paper towels (reserve milk in skillet for custard); chill the meringues well.
● Meanwhile, for the custard, in a medium saucepan combine the beaten egg yolks and the 2 tablespoons sugar. Measure the reserved milk; add enough additional milk to make 1½ cups. Stir milk into the yolk mixture.
● Cook and stir over low heat till mixture thickens slightly and coats a metal spoon. Remove from heat. Cool custard quickly by placing the saucepan in a sink or bowl of ice water and stirring for 1 to 2 minutes. Stir in vanilla and nutmeg, if desired.
● Spoon desired fresh fruit into 6 serving dishes. Spoon the custard over fruit. Top each serving with a chilled meringue. Makes 6 servings.

***Fruit Options:** Choose one or any combination of the following: Peeled and sliced or cut-up bananas, kiwi fruit, melon, papayas, or peaches; sliced or cut-up apricots, nectarines, or plums; peeled and sectioned oranges or tangerines; or berries (halve large strawberries).

Berries 'n' Cream Torte

If you're in a hurry, replace the frozen filling with 1 quart of your favorite ice cream.

1   14-ounce can (1¼ cups)
      sweetened condensed
      milk
⅓ cup lemon juice
1   pint fresh strawberries,
      mashed (1⅓ cups)
1   cup whipping cream
½ cup coarsely chopped
      almonds, toasted
1   11-ounce package 3-inch
      soft apple spice *or*
      oatmeal cookies
3   tablespoons sugar
2   teaspoons cornstarch
½ cup unsweetened pineapple
      juice
1   tablespoon brandy
      (optional)
2   cups desired berries

● For strawberry filling, in a mixing bowl combine sweetened condensed milk and lemon juice; stir just till mixture begins to thicken. Stir mashed strawberries into milk mixture. Beat whipping cream just till it mounds; fold into berry mixture. Cover and freeze till firm. Break up frozen mixture and place in a chilled mixer bowl; beat with an electric mixer till smooth. Fold in chopped almonds.

● For the torte, line a 2-quart soufflé dish with clear plastic wrap, extending wrap 2 to 3 inches above dish. Gently press 7 or 8 cookies around the inside of dish, overlapping to form a scalloped edge. Place about *half* of the remaining cookies on the bottom of dish, breaking cookies as necessary to fit.

● Spoon *half* of the strawberry filling over cookies in bottom of dish. Arrange remaining cookies on top. Spoon on the remaining strawberry filling. Seal, label, and freeze.

● **To serve,** for sauce, in a small saucepan combine sugar and cornstarch. Stir in pineapple juice. Cook and stir till thickened and bubbly, then cook and stir 2 minutes more. Remove from heat; stir in brandy. Cover surface with clear plastic wrap. Cool.

● Remove frozen torte from dish by pulling up on plastic wrap; carefully remove plastic wrap. Transfer torte to a serving platter. Top with desired berries; spoon sauce over the berries. Makes 8 to 10 servings.

1 Assembling the ice cream torte

After lining the dish with plastic wrap, press 7 or 8 cookies around the inside of the dish. Overlap the cookies in the dish to form a scalloped edge. Place half of the remaining cookies in the bottom of the dish. You might have to break some of the cookies to fit. Spoon half of the strawberry filling over the cookies in the bottom of the dish and arrange the remaining cookies on top. Then top with the remaining strawberry filling.

2 Serving the ice cream torte

After removing the frozen torte from the soufflé dish and discarding the plastic wrap, arrange desired berries on top. Carefully spoon the sauce over the berries, letting some of the sauce run down the sides of the torte.

If fresh berries are not available, use frozen fruit instead. Thaw and drain the frozen fruit before placing it on the torte.

Index